Profiles of the Presidents

GERALD R. FORD

★ ★ ★

Profiles of the Presidents

GERALD R. FORD

by Andrew Santella

Content Adviser: Jim Kratsas, De████████████████████ Museum, Grand Rapids, Michigan

Reading Adviser: Dr. Linda D. Labbo, Department of Reading Education, College of Education, The University of Georgia

COMPASS POINT BOOKS MINNEAPOLIS, MINNESOTA

Compass Point Books
3109 West 50th Street, #115
Minneapolis, MN 55410

Visit Compass Point Books on the Internet at *www.compasspointbooks.com*
or e-mail your request to *custserv@compasspointbooks.com*

Editors: E. Russell Primm, Emily J. Dolbear, Melissa McDaniel, and Catherine Neitge
Photo Researcher: Svetlana Zhurkina
Photo Selector: Linda S. Koutris
Designer: The Design Lab
Cartographer: XNR Productions, Inc.

Library of Congress Cataloging-in-Publication Data
  Santella, Andrew.
  Gerald R. Ford / by Andrew Santella.
      p. cm. — (Profiles of the presidents)
Summary: A biography of the thirty-eighth president of the United States, discussing his personal life, education, and political career.
Includes bibliographical references and index.
  ISBN 0-7565-0282-9 (hardcover : alk. paper)
  1. Ford, Gerald R., 1913– —Juvenile literature. 2. Presidents—United States—Biography—
Juvenile literature. [1. Ford, Gerald R., 1913– 2. Presidents.] I. Title. II. Series.
  E866.S26 2003
  973.925'092—dc21   2002153303

Table of Contents

★ ★ ★

*NOTE: In this book, words that are defined in the glossary are in **bold** the first time they appear in the text.*

"I Will Not Let You Down"

★ ★ ★

President Richard Nixon, with his wife, Pat, saying farewell to his staff and cabinet after resigning from office in 1974

The president had some urgent news. On August 8, 1974, President Richard Nixon told Vice President Gerald Ford that he wanted to see him. Ford hurried to the president's office. When he arrived, the president came right to the point.

"I have made the decision to resign," Nixon told Ford. He was going to leave the presidency. "It's in the best interest of the country," Nixon said.

The news was no surprise to Ford. Nixon stood accused of serious crimes. He had lied to the American people and misused the power of the presidency. He had tried to cover up his own crimes and crimes committed by his staff and supporters. Congress was ready to **impeach** Nixon for his actions and force him from office. Nixon chose to resign rather than endure the shame of being impeached.

Never before had an American president resigned his office. Never before had the American people's faith in government been so badly shaken.

When Nixon resigned, Ford would become president. It would be up to him to restore the public's faith in government. He knew it would be no easy task. However, he told Nixon, "I am ready to do the job, and I think I am fully qualified to do it."

Not everyone was so sure that Ford was up to the job. He had been vice president for only eight months. In 1973, Ford was chosen by Nixon and approved by Congress to replace Vice President Spiro Agnew. He had resigned after being accused of accepting **bribes.** Now

▼ *Ford (left) and Nixon in 1973*

Ford was taking Nixon's place as president. He was the first person to become president without being elected either president or vice president. Even though American voters had not elected him, they looked to him to heal the wounds left by the crimes of the Nixon presidency.

Ford's term as president began the next day, August 9, 1974. Many people gathered in the East Room of the White House to watch Ford take the presidential oath of office. Millions more watched on television. "I will not let you down," Ford promised the American people. It was up to him to get Americans to trust their government again.

Betty Ford looks ▶
on as her
husband (left)
is sworn into
office on
August 9, 1974.

Troubled Start, Promising Future

★ ★ ★

The thirty-eighth president of the United States was born on July 14, 1913, in Omaha, Nebraska. Although the world would come to know him as Gerald Ford, he was born Leslie Lynch King Jr. His parents had a troubled marriage. His mother, Dorothy, was abused by his father. Shortly after she gave birth, Dorothy made up her mind to leave her violent husband and divorce him. She took her infant son with her. Mother and child moved to Grand Rapids, Michigan. There, Dorothy met

▾ *Gerald (then Leslie Lynch) and his mother in September 1913*

Ford graduated ▲ from high school in 1931.

and married a paint store owner named Gerald Rudolph Ford. Dorothy's two-year-old son took the name of his adoptive father. In time, the Fords would have three more sons.

Despite his difficult start, young Gerald soon settled into a happy childhood in Grand Rapids. He played football, joined the Boy Scouts, and did well in school. He was a star center for the South High School football team and was voted the most popular boy in his senior class. He worked part-time jobs at a local diner and a nearby amusement park. He also studied hard and graduated near the top of his class.

Ford wanted to attend college, but money was scarce for the Ford family. His father's paint business was struggling. In fact, the entire country was facing hard times during the 1930s. It was the height of the Great Depression, a severe economic crisis that left many people without jobs or homes.

Ford's teachers and neighbors saw great promise in him. They were determined to help him get a college education. With financial help from friends in Grand Rapids, Ford was able to attend the University of Michigan. He worked his way through school waiting on tables. Ford studied economics and political science. He also continued to play football. In his senior year at Michigan, Ford was voted the team's most valuable player. He graduated in 1935, and both the Detroit Lions and the Green Bay Packers offered him contracts to play professional football.

Ford had other plans. He wanted to attend law school. However, he still needed to earn money to pay for his schooling. Ford took a job as a football

▾ *Ford was a star football player at the University of Michigan.*

Coach Ford (back row, third from left) with the Yale University boxing team in 1936

and boxing coach at Yale University, and he began studying at Yale Law School. He spent the next few years juggling his duties as an assistant football coach and as a law student. Somehow, Ford managed to pull it off. He graduated from law school in 1941.

He returned home to Michigan and passed the tests that allowed him to practice law there. He started a law firm with with Philip Buchen, a friend from the University of Michigan. The new firm of Ford and

Buchen soon had many clients, and the partners were kept busy. It wasn't long, however, before Ford's law career was interrupted by world events. In December 1941, Japan attacked the U.S. naval base at Pearl Harbor in Hawaii. The United States declared war and entered World War II (1939–1945).

▼ *The USS* Shaw *was one of the many ships destroyed in the Japanese attack on Pearl Harbor.*

Entering the World of Politics

★ ★ ★

Ford joined the U.S. Navy in April 1942. Because he was a talented athlete, he was given a job as a physical fitness instructor at a navy flight school in North Carolina. Ford

Ford rose from the ▼ rank of navy ensign to lieutenant commander during World War II.

wanted to be involved in the fighting. He kept writing letters to people above him in rank, asking to be sent overseas. Finally they agreed. He was sent to work on the aircraft carrier USS *Monterey.*

Ford served on the *Monterey* in the South Pacific from June 1943 until December 1944. He took part in several major battles, including Wake Island,

To work for YOU in CONGRESS

GERALD R. FORD JR.

REPUBLICAN PRIMARY SEPT. 14

UNITED STATES REPRESENTATIVE

WALKER & CO.

▲ *A billboard used in Ford's 1948 campaign for the U.S. House of Representatives*

Okinawa, and the Battle of the Philippines. Ford left the navy in 1946, the year after the war ended. He had reached the rank of lieutenant commander.

After the war, he returned to Grand Rapids to practice law in the city's top law firm—Butterfield, Keeney and Amberg. He also set a new goal for himself: Ford wanted to win election to the U.S. House of Representatives. He had set a difficult challenge for himself. Ford would have to defeat the congressman who already held

Betty and Gerald ▶
Ford on their
wedding day
in 1948

the office, Bartel Jonkman. What's more, Jonkman had the support of many of Michigan's most powerful Republicans.

Just before he ran for Congress, Ford began dating Elizabeth Ann "Betty" Bloomer. She was a thirty-year-old former dancer who worked as a fashion expert for a Grand Rapids department store. Her first marriage had ended in divorce after five years. On October 15, 1948, the two were married at Grace Episcopal Church in Grand Rapids. Unfortunately, there was no time for a honeymoon. By now, the election was a month away. Right after the wedding, Ford was back on the **campaign** trail.

Few people had given the young lawyer much of a chance to win the election. That only made Ford work harder. He attended rallies, made speeches, and shook thousands of hands. His hard work paid off. He had defeated Jonkman to become the Republican **candidate.** Then he won a huge victory over the Democratic candidate. The young man from Grand Rapids was now Congressman Ford.

Heading to Washington

★ ★ ★

Ford was one of the few new Republicans to win election to Congress in 1948. Democrat Harry Truman was elected president that year, and Democrats swept to power in both houses of Congress.

On January 3, 1949, Gerald Ford was sworn in as a member of Congress. His wife of eleven weeks, Betty, watched proudly from the balcony of the House of Representatives. Ford decided he wanted to spend his career serving as a member of the House of Representatives.

He moved into his new offices and began to

Gerald Ford with his parents, Dorothy and Gerald Ford Sr., in 1948 ▾

meet other members of Congress. Down the hall was John
F. Kennedy, a young congressman from Massachusetts.
Also making a name for himself there was a Californian
named Richard M. Nixon. All three congressmen—and
future presidents—had served in the navy during World
War II. They liked to swap stories about their time in the
service. Ford and Nixon became especially good friends.

The Fords grew to enjoy their new life in Washington.
They welcomed their first son, Michael, in 1950. Two
more sons soon followed. John was born in 1952, and

▾ *Ford became friends with Richard Nixon (back row, far right) and John F. Kennedy (back row, second from right), shown here with other newly elected congressmen in Washington, D.C., in 1947.*

The Ford family ▲
in 1959

Steven in 1956. Their only daughter, Susan, was born in 1957.

During Ford's first term in the House, he was chosen to sit on the powerful **committee** that controls how the federal government spends money. Ford would eventually serve twenty-five years in Congress. During that time, he slowly gained experience and influence until he became one of the most powerful Republicans in Washington. In 1963, he was elected chairman of the House Republican Conference, making him a national party leader.

That same year, his old friend John F. Kennedy, who had become president, was shot and killed. Ford was one of two House members named to a special committee investigating the murder. In 1965, Ford became the House minority leader—the top Republican member of the House of Representatives.

▼ *Senate Minority Leader Everett M. Dirksen raising Ford's hand after Ford's election as House minority leader*

President Lyndon B. Johnson's policies were often criticized by Ford.

As Ford's power grew, he remained loyal to the Republican Party and its other leaders. He had supported Republican President Dwight Eisenhower during his two terms in the White House in the 1950s. He was a leading critic of Democratic President Lyndon Baines Johnson, who served from 1963 to 1969. At that time, the United States was involved in a war in the Southeast Asian country of Vietnam. Ford criticized Johnson's handling of the Vietnam War (1959–1975). He thought Johnson was acting with too much restraint. He said the president should use the full military power of the United States to win the war. Ford also attacked many of Johnson's policies to improve education and reduce poverty in the United States. Ford claimed that Johnson's policies would not work and would only be more expensive for the American people.

Ford had long been a close friend of Richard Nixon. After Nixon was elected president in 1968, Ford was one of his most loyal supporters. Ford worked hard to win votes in Congress that would help turn Nixon's political ideas into laws.

His loyalty to Nixon led to one of Ford's worst political mistakes. Ford led an attempt in 1970 to impeach Supreme Court Justice William O. Douglas. Douglas was one of Nixon's political enemies. He often made decisions that Ford and Nixon disagreed with. Ford claimed that the judge had not acted **ethically** and should be removed from the Court. Few members of Congress agreed. Ford was widely criticized for trying

▼ *Supreme Court Justice William O. Douglas made decisions that Ford and Nixon did not always agree with.*

Ford, shown here ▲ speaking on television, had planned to retire after one final congressional election in 1974.

to impeach Douglas, and the move failed.

After more than two decades in the House of Representatives and the criticism he received for the attempted impeachment of Douglas, Ford began to look forward to retirement. His busy life as a congressman left him little time for his family. Betty Ford struggled to handle the demanding and lonely life of a congressman's wife. Ford decided that he would retire after running for Congress once more in 1974. Before this final election, however, Ford would be called to take on an even bigger responsibility.

Serving His Nation

★ ★ ★

On June 17, 1972, five men were caught breaking into Democratic Party headquarters at the Watergate apartments in Washington, D.C. At first, it appeared to be an ordinary burglary attempt. However, over time it became clear that the burglars were following orders given by people close to President Nixon. The president claimed to know nothing about the break-in, but many Americans doubted him. As

▸ *The Judiciary Committee Impeachment Panel meeting in July 1974 to hear evidence of Nixon's involvement with Watergate*

MR. RODINO
CHAIRMAN

NOHUE

Mr. HUTCHINSON

the Watergate scandal grew, Ford continued to stand by the president and to speak in his defense.

Watergate was not Nixon's only problem. His vice president, Spiro Agnew, had been accused of taking bribes while he was governor of Maryland during the 1960s. According to the Justice Department, Agnew continued to accept bribes even after he was vice president. On October 10, 1973, Agnew was forced to resign.

Nixon had to choose a replacement for Agnew. His choice had to be approved by both the Senate and the House of

Nixon with his first vice president, Spiro Agnew, in December 1968

Ford being ▸ sworn in as vice president in December 1973

Representatives. With talk of political **corruption** every-where in the news, Nixon needed a vice president known for his honesty. He chose Gerald Ford. Nixon knew that Ford was well respected by members of Congress. He figured that Ford would win easy approval.

He was right. The Senate approved Ford by a vote of 92 to 3. In the House of Representatives, the vote was 387 to 35. On December 6, 1973, Ford was sworn in as vice president of the United States.

As vice president, Ford had few formal duties. Nixon depended on a small number of aides and advisers. He rarely involved Ford in important decisions. Despite this,

◄ *Vice President Ford speaking to Republicans in San Diego in July 1974*

Ford continued to
support Nixon even
after the Watergate
scandal broke.

Ford remained loyal to Nixon. He traveled around the country, giving speeches and defending Nixon's performance as president. Nixon continued to claim that he had nothing to do with the Watergate scandal, and Ford believed him. Ford stuck up for the president, while most others were attacking Nixon.

Even Ford soon realized, however, that Nixon had been lying when he said he had nothing to do with Watergate. In the summer of 1974, new evidence proved that Nixon had tried to cover up crimes committed by people working in the White House. He had even used the power of the presidency to try to order the Federal Bureau of Investigation

(FBI) not to investigate the crimes. When this new evidence was made public, it became clear that Nixon could no longer be president. If he didn't resign, Congress would certainly impeach him and force him from office.

This meant that Ford would take Nixon's place as president of the United States. On August 1, 1974, Nixon's chief of staff, Alexander Haig, visited Ford. Haig told Ford that Nixon would consider resigning right away if Ford would promise something in return. Nixon wanted Ford to **pardon** him—or clear him of any responsibility for crimes he committed as president. Once Ford became president, he would have the power to make such a pardon. Nixon wanted him to promise to do so ahead of time. Ford thought about it briefly. Then he refused to make such a promise.

Despite Ford's refusal, Nixon did resign. He went on national television on August 8, 1974, to announce that he

▲ *Alexander Haig asked Ford to pardon Nixon for his involvement in Watergate.*

was leaving office the next day. Meanwhile, Ford's staff was rushing to plan for his **inauguration** on August 9. Invitations were sent to key members of Congress, other top figures in American politics, and important foreign officials. Chief Justice Warren Burger hurried home from a trip to Europe to conduct the inauguration.

Son-in-law David Eisenhower watches as Nixon says good-bye to his staff at the White House in August 1974.

Early on the morning of August 9, Nixon said good-bye to his staff. He signed his official letter of resignation and boarded a plane to return home to California. The inauguration of Gerald Ford began just past noon. When

he and his wife, Betty, walked into the East Room of the White House, the people there gave him a standing ovation. Ford repeated the oath read to him by Chief Justice Burger and became the thirty-eighth president.

Then Ford delivered a short speech that was broadcast on television across the nation. He asked his audience not to think of it as an inaugural address, the speech a newly sworn-in president gives about his hopes for his presidency. Instead, Ford wanted people to think of it as "just a little straight talk among friends." He

▲ *Ford and his wife, Betty, during the swearing-in ceremony conducted by Chief Justice Warren Burger*

Ford addressing guests in the East Room of the White House after his inauguration ▶

wanted the nation to know that he understood their anger and disappointment over Nixon's actions. "This is an hour of history that troubles our minds and hurts our hearts," he said. Ford pledged he would work to "bind up the internal wounds of Watergate." It was time to move forward again. "Our long national nightmare is over," Ford declared.

President Ford

★ ★ ★

Ford's first and most difficult task as president was to restore the people's confidence in their government. In his first week as president, he made a rare visit to Congress to deliver a speech before members of the House of Representatives and the Senate. He promised to speak openly and honestly to the American people.

▾ *Ford delivering a speech to Congress*

Henry Kissinger ▸ continued to serve as secretary of state under Ford.

Ford found it hard ▾ to gain the public's trust early in his term, especially after he pardoned former president Nixon. Here Ford is shown defending his decision to grant the pardon during a September 1974 press conference.

At the same time, Ford was choosing **cabinet** members. He kept some of Nixon's advisers. He asked Henry Kissinger to stay on as secretary of state. He also kept Secretary of the Treasury William Simon and Secretary of Agriculture Earl Butz. Ford replaced the rest of Nixon's cabinet with his own choices. Finally, Ford chose Governor Nelson A. Rockefeller of New York to act as vice president.

Earning the public's trust proved difficult for Ford. The trouble began just one month after he became president. On September 8, 1974, Ford granted "a full, free and

absolute pardon" to former president Nixon "for all offenses" he had committed while he was president. This meant that Nixon could not be punished for any of his crimes.

Ford came under intense criticism for this pardon. He believed, however, that he had good reason for doing it. He knew that any trial of Nixon would drag on for months and even years. A trial would only prolong the bitterness of the Watergate scandal. Ford believed it was time for the nation to leave the scandal behind and move on to new business. He also believed that Nixon had suffered enough by leaving the presidency in disgrace.

▲ *The front page of the* Washington Star-News *told of Nixon's resignation in August 1974. By September, Ford believed it was time for Americans to leave the scandal behind them.*

The pardon angered many Americans. Coming so soon in the Ford presidency, it appeared that the pardon was just another part of the effort to cover up Watergate crimes. To many, it looked like Ford issued the pardon in exchange for the chance to become president. Ford's own press secretary quit because of the pardon.

In response to the criticism, Ford did something remarkable. He went to Capitol Hill to answer questions about the pardon asked by a committee of the House of

Representatives. It was the first time in history that a president had answered questions under oath for a congressional investigation.

Ford's answers satisfied the committee, and some of the criticism of the pardon died down. However, American voters never forgot Ford's part in pardoning Richard Nixon.

Ford's job was made more difficult by problems in the American economy. The prices of goods were rising rapidly. This is called inflation. At the same time, the economy was slowing down, or entering a recession. Fewer people were making major purchases such as new cars or homes. More people were losing their jobs. By early 1975, nearly one in

◀ These women heading toward an employment office in Baltimore, Maryland, in the 1970s were among many Americans looking for work at that time.

ten American workers was without a job. This combination of recession and inflation is rare, and it made life difficult for many Americans during Ford's administration.

U.S. Marines ▾ crossing the Vu Gia River in Vietnam in 1969

Ford focused on stopping inflation. He promoted the saying "Whip Inflation Now," or WIN. He was unable to do much to improve the economy, however. Congress was controlled by Democrats who disagreed with Ford's policies. They wanted to spend money to create new jobs for workers. Ford wanted to reduce government spending. With Congress and the president at odds, little was done to end the hard times for ordinary people.

Ford became president as the United States was trying to end its involvement in the Vietnam War. For more than ten years, American troops had tried to help the government of South Vietnam defeat forces from North Vietnam. North Vietnam was communist, meaning that the government controlled businesses and the economy. By 1974, it was clear that the communist forces would win. This would be an embarrassing defeat for the American military.

The Vietnam War was unpopular in the United States. Many young people went into hiding or fled to other countries to avoid being drafted, or forced to serve in the military. In 1974, Ford offered amnesty—or protection against

▼ *These young men fled to Canada to avoid being drafted during the Vietnam War.*

Secretary of State Henry Kissinger (left) and National Security Adviser Brent Scowcroft (far right) discuss the situation in Saigon with President Ford in April 1975.

punishment—to all who had avoided the draft or had run away from the military. Ford hoped this would be the first step in helping the nation get over the bitterness of the war.

The war finally ended in 1975 when North Vietnamese forces took over the South Vietnamese capital of Saigon. The last American troops and government officials left Saigon on April 29, 1975.

Communist forces also gained control of the neighboring countries of Laos and Cambodia. On May 12, 1975,

Cambodian forces captured the American cargo ship
Mayaguez and its crew. Ford ordered a rescue effort.
The thirty-nine crew members were soon released
unharmed, but forty-one American soldiers died in the
effort to win their release.

Working with Secretary of State Kissinger, Ford tried
to improve relations with the world's two major communist
powers, the Soviet Union and China. Ford traveled to both

▼ *The* Mayaguez *after
Cambodian forces
released the ship
and its crew in
May 1975*

countries during his presidency. He also tried unsuccessfully to work out agreements that would limit the number of nuclear weapons each nation could have. Just one of these powerful bombs can cause widespread destruction. Even though he tried to limit nuclear weapons overseas, Ford also called on Congress to spend more money on the military.

Ford speaks with ▲ Soviet General Secretary Leonid Brezhnev during a trip to the Soviet Union in November 1974.

Chinese communist ▶ leader Mao Tse Tung with Ford in China in December 1975

In Ford's second year as president, two different people tried to kill him within a few weeks. On September 5, 1975, twenty-six-year-old Lynette "Squeaky" Fromme pointed a gun at the president as he greeted crowds in Sacramento, California. She was captured before she could harm him. Fromme was later convicted and sentenced to life in prison. Less than three weeks later in San Francisco, California, Sara Jane Moore fired a gun at the president, but he was not harmed. She, too, was captured, convicted, and sentenced to life in prison.

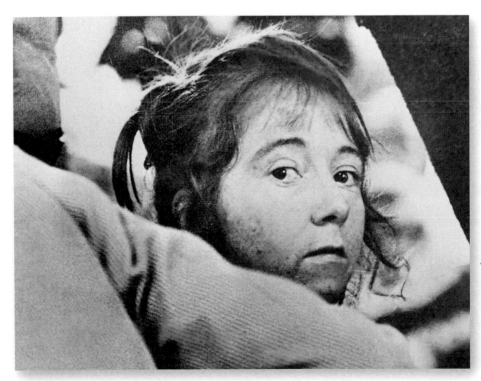

◀ *Lynette Fromme pointed a gun at President Ford in Sacramento, California, in September 1975.*

Life After the White House

★ ★ ★

Nancy and Ronald Reagan (left) with President Ford and Vice President Rockefeller (right) at the 1976 Republican National Convention

Not long after he became president, Ford decided that he would run for president in 1976. First, he had to win the support of his own Republican Party. Normally, presidents get the full support of their own party and easily become their party's candidate for president. Ford believed that he had performed well enough by 1976 to be nominated.

However, former California governor Ronald Reagan also wanted to be the Republican candidate. The race between Ford and Reagan was surpris-

ingly close, but Ford managed to earn his party's support. He chose Senator Robert Dole of Kansas as his vice presidential running mate.

As the Republican candidate, Ford had to take on Democrat Jimmy Carter, a former governor of Georgia. Carter was almost unknown outside Georgia when he began his run for the White House. That turned out to be an advantage for Carter. After the Watergate scandal, voters did not trust Washington politicians. They were ready for a change, and Carter represented change.

◄ *Running mates Jimmy Carter (left) and Walter Mondale at the Democratic National Convention in 1976*

Many voters saw Ford as part of Nixon's team. They also remembered how Ford had pardoned Nixon.

Carter had a huge lead early in the campaign, but Ford refused to give up. He campaigned hard and eventually made the race very close. Ford's determination

Rosalyn Carter (left) ▶ and Betty Ford with husbands Gerald Ford and Jimmy Carter in November 1976, shortly after Carter's victory over Ford

was not enough, however. Carter won the election. It was the first defeat Ford had suffered in his twenty-eight years in politics.

First Lady Betty Ford took her husband's loss especially hard. In her two and a half years as first lady, she had been very popular. She spoke out in favor of women's rights and urged her husband to appoint women to top government positions.

▲ *First Lady Betty Ford in 1976*

Betty Ford had a difficult time adjusting to life after the White House. She began drinking too much and became addicted to pills. Finally, she checked into the Alcohol and Drug Rehabilitation Center of Long Beach Naval Hospital to get help. When she was well again, she wrote a book about her experience, hoping to help others with similar problems. In 1982, she opened the Betty Ford Center for Drug and Alcohol Rehabilitation in Rancho Mirage, California. In 1991, President George H. W. Bush awarded Betty Ford the Presidential Medal of Freedom, one of the nation's highest honors, for her work helping people overcome drug and alcohol problems.

After leaving the White House, the Fords settled in Palm Springs, California. Gerald Ford never again ran for public office, though there was some talk that he might become Ronald Reagan's vice presidential candidate in the

1974: Becomes 38th president of the United States after President Nixon resigns

1913: Born in Omaha, Nebraska

Gerald R. Ford Museum

University of Michigan and Gerald R. Ford Library

Serves in Congress for 25 years before being nominated by President Nixon to replace Vice President Spiro Angew, after Agnew resigns amid bribery charges

Serves in the Navy during WWII on the aircraft carrier USS Monterey

300 mi.

300 km

◄ Former president
Gerald Ford with
golfer Jack Nicklaus
(left) at a golf
tournament in
Pebble Beach,
California, during
the 1980s

1980 election. Instead, Ford lived the active life of a respected retired politician. He gave speeches all over the world and sometimes served as an official representative of the United States.

Although his brief time as president was a difficult one, Gerald Ford came to be remembered as an honest man who tried to see his nation through the crisis of Watergate. In 1999, President Bill Clinton awarded

Ford the Presidential Medal of Freedom for his service as president. The award recognized all Ford had done twenty-five years earlier to lead the United States out of its "national nightmare."

Ford was awarded ▶
the Presidential
Medal of Freedom
in 1999.

GERALD R. FORD

GLOSSARY

★ ★ ★

bribes—money given illegally to influence someone else's opinions or actions

cabinet—a president's group of advisers who are heads of government departments

campaign—an organized effort to win an election

candidate—someone running for office in an election

committee—a group of people working together on a project

corruption—willingness to do things that are wrong or illegal

ethically—having to do with right and wrong behavior

impeach—to charge a public official with a serious crime

inauguration—a president's swearing-in ceremony

pardon—act that forgives a crime, so that the person who committed the crime is not punished

GERALD R. FORD'S LIFE AT A GLANCE

★ ★ ★

PERSONAL

Nickname: Jerry

Birth date: July 14, 1913

Birthplace: Omaha, Nebraska

Birth father's name: Leslie Lynch King Sr.

Adoptive father's name: Gerald R. Ford Sr.

Mother's name: Dorothy Gardner King Ford

Education: Graduated from University of Michigan in 1935; graduated from Yale Law School in 1941

Wife's name: Elizabeth Ann Bloomer Ford (1918–)

Married: October 15, 1948

Children: Michael Gerald Ford (1950–); John Gardner Ford (1952–); Steven Meigs Ford (1956–); Susan Elizabeth Ford (1957–)

PUBLIC

Occupation before presidency:	Lawyer, politician
Occupation after presidency:	None
Military service:	U.S. Navy during World War II
Other government positions:	Representative from Michigan in the U.S. House of Representatives; vice president
Political party:	Republican
Vice president:	Nelson A. Rockefeller, (1974–1977)
Dates in office:	August 9, 1974–January 20, 1977
Presidential opponent:	James Earl Carter Jr. (Democrat), 1976
Number of votes (Electoral College):	39,145,977 of 79,973,373 (240 of 538)
Writings:	*A Time to Heal* (1979)

Gerald R. Ford's Cabinet

Secretary of state:
  Henry A. Kissinger (1974–1977)

Secretary of the treasury:
  William E. Simon (1974–1977)

Secretary of defense:
  James R. Schlesinger (1974–1975)
  Donald H. Rumsfeld (1975–1977)

Attorney general:
  William B. Saxbe (1974–1975)
  Edward H. Levi (1975–1977)

Secretary of the interior:
  Rogers C. B. Morton (1974–1975)
  Stanley K. Hathaway (1975)
  Thomas S. Kleppe (1975–1977)

Secretary of agriculture:
  Earl L. Butz (1974–1976)
  John A. Knebel (1976–1977)

Secretary of commerce:
  Frederick B. Dent (1974–1975)
  Rogers C. D. Morton (1975)
  Elliot L. Richardson (1975–1977)

Secretary of labor:
  Peter J. Brennan (1974–1975)
  John T. Dunlop (1975–1976)
  W. J. Usery Jr. (1976–1977)

Secretary of health, education, and welfare:
  Caspar W. Weinberger (1974–1975)
  F. David Matthews (1975–1977)

Secretary of housing and urban development:
  James T. Lynn (1974–1975)
  Carla Anderson Hills (1975–1977)

Secretary of transportation:
  Claude S. Brinegar (1974–1975)
  William T. Coleman Jr. (1975–1977)

GERALD R. FORD'S LIFE AND TIMES

★ ★ ★

FORD'S LIFE

WORLD EVENTS

1910

July 14, Ford is born in Omaha, Nebraska, originally named Leslie Lynch King Jr. **1913**

1913 Henry Ford begins to use standard assembly lines to produce automobiles

Adopted by his mother's second husband, Gerald Rudolph Ford, and renamed after him **1916**

1916 German-born physicist Albert Einstein (above) publishes his general theory of relativity

1920 1920 American women get the right to vote

1926 A.A. Milne publishes *Winnie the Pooh*

FORD'S LIFE

Graduates from high 1931
school (below)

Graduates from the 1935
University of Michigan

Graduates from Yale 1941
Law School

Enters the U.S. 1942
Navy (below)

Marries Elizabeth 1948
Ann Bloomer

Elected to the U.S.
House of
Representatives

1930

1940

1950

WORLD EVENTS

1933   Nazi leader Adolf
Hitler (above) is
named chancellor
of Germany

1935   George Gershwin's
opera *Porgy and Bess*
opens in New York

1941   December 7, Japanese
bombers attack Pearl
Harbor, Hawaii
(below), and America
enters World War II

1955   Disneyland, the first
theme part in the
United States, opens in
Anaheim, California

FORD'S LIFE		WORLD EVENTS

1960

1960   Civil rights sit-ins begin in North Carolina and spread across the South

1961   The Berlin Wall is built, dividing East and West Germany (below)

Named to a special   1963
committee
investigating the
murder of President
John F. Kennedy

1963   Dr. Martin Luther King Jr. delivers his "I Have a Dream" speech to more than 250,000 people attending the March on Washington

Becomes House   1965
minority leader (below)

1967   The first heart transplant is attempted

1968   Civil rights leader Martin Luther King Jr. (below) is assassinated

FORD'S LIFE

Leads an effort to   1970
impeach Supreme
Court Justice William
O. Douglas

June 17, five men are   1972
caught breaking into
the Democratic Party
headquarters,
beginning the
Watergate scandal

Vice President Spiro   1973
Agnew resigns;
President Richard
Nixon chooses Ford to
replace him (above)

1970

WORLD EVENTS

1970   Earth Day is
celebrated for the first
time, promoting
environmental
awareness worldwide

The *Apollo 13* space
mission is launched
from Cape Kennedy,
Florida

1971   The first micro-
processor is produced
by Intel (below)

1973   Spanish artist Pablo
Picasso (below) dies

FORD'S LIFE		WORLD EVENTS
August 9, President Richard Nixon resigns; Ford is sworn in as the new president, becoming the only president to not be elected either vice president or president	**1974**	**1974** Scientists find that chlorofluorocarbons— chemicals in coolants and propellants—are damaging to Earth's ozone layer

September 8, Ford pardons Nixon for all crimes he may have committed as president (left)

1975 April 29, the last American troops and officials leave Vietnam

September 5, Lynette Fromme attempts to kill Ford in Sacramento, California

September 22, Sara Jane Moore attempts to kill Ford in San Francisco, California

1976 Ford loses the presidential election to Jimmy Carter (below right)

1976 U.S. military academies admit women (above)

1978 The first test-tube baby conceived outside its mother's womb is born in Oldham, England

FORD'S LIFE

WORLD EVENTS

Publishes his
autobiography,
A Time to Heal

1979

1980

Betty Ford Center
for Drug and
Alcohol Rehabilitation
opens in Rancho
Mirage, California

1982

1982

Maya Lin designs the
Vietnam War
Memorial (right),
commemorating the
Americans who died

1990

1990

Political prisoner
Nelson Mandela
(right), a leader of
the antiapartheid
movement in South
Africa, is released;
Mandela becomes
president of South
Africa in 1994

Betty Ford (above)
awarded the
Presidential Medal
of Freedom

1991

1991

Conflict between Iraq
and Kuwait in the
Persian Gulf begins

1994

Genocide of 500,000
to 1 million of the
minority Tutsi group
by rival Hutu people
occurs in Rwanda

1996

A sheep is cloned in
Scotland

Awarded the
Presidential Medal of
Freedom (above)

1999

UNDERSTANDING GERALD R. FORD AND HIS PRESIDENCY

★ ★ ★

IN THE LIBRARY

Cohen, Daniel. *Watergate: Deception in the White House.*
Brookfield, Conn.: Millbrook Press, 1998.

Francis, Sandra. *Gerald Ford: Our Thirty-Eighth President.*
Chanhassen, Minn.: The Child's World, 2002.

Joseph, Paul. *Gerald Ford.* Edina, Minn.: Abdo Publishing, 2000.

ON THE WEB

For more information on *Gerald R. Ford,* use FactHound to track
down Web sites related to this book.

1. Go to *www.facthound.com*

2. Type in this book ID: 0756502829

3. Click on the *Fetch It* button.

Your trusty FactHound will fetch the best Web sites for you!

FORD HISTORIC SITES
ACROSS THE COUNTRY

Ford Birthsite and Gardens
Nebraska State Historical Society
3202 Woolworth Avenue
Omaha, NE 68103
402/444-5900
To visit Ford's birthplace

Gerald R. Ford Exhibit
Gerald R. Ford
Conservation Center
1326 South 32nd Street
Omaha, NE 68105
402/595-1180
To see exhibits about Ford's birth and career

Gerald R. Ford Library
1000 Beal Avenue
Ann Arbor, MI 48109
734/741-2218
To learn more about
Ford's life and times

Gerald R. Ford Museum
303 Pearl Street N.W.
Grand Rapids, MI 49504
616/451-9263
To view exhibits on the life, career,
and presidency of Ford

THE U.S. PRESIDENTS
(Years in Office)

★ ★ ★

1. **George Washington**
    (March 4, 1789–March 3, 1797)
2. **John Adams**
    (March 4, 1797–March 3, 1801)
3. **Thomas Jefferson**
    (March 4, 1801–March 3, 1809)
4. **James Madison**
    (March 4, 1809–March 3, 1817)
5. **James Monroe**
    (March 4, 1817–March 3, 1825)
6. **John Quincy Adams**
    (March 4, 1825–March 3, 1829)
7. **Andrew Jackson**
    (March 4, 1829–March 3, 1837)
8. **Martin Van Buren**
    (March 4, 1837–March 3, 1841)
9. **William Henry Harrison**
    (March 6, 1841–April 4, 1841)
10. **John Tyler**
    (April 6, 1841–March 3, 1845)
11. **James K. Polk**
    (March 4, 1845–March 3, 1849)
12. **Zachary Taylor**
    (March 5, 1849–July 9, 1850)
13. **Millard Fillmore**
    (July 10, 1850–March 3, 1853)
14. **Franklin Pierce**
    (March 4, 1853–March 3, 1857)
15. **James Buchanan**
    (March 4, 1857–March 3, 1861)
16. **Abraham Lincoln**
    (March 4, 1861–April 15, 1865)
17. **Andrew Johnson**
    (April 15, 1865–March 3, 1869)

18. **Ulysses S. Grant**
    (March 4, 1869–March 3, 1877)
19. **Rutherford B. Hayes**
    (March 4, 1877–March 3, 1881)
20. **James Garfield**
    (March 4, 1881–Sept 19, 1881)
21. **Chester Arthur**
    (Sept 20, 1881–March 3, 1885)
22. **Grover Cleveland**
    (March 4, 1885–March 3, 1889)
23. **Benjamin Harrison**
    (March 4, 1889–March 3, 1893)
24. **Grover Cleveland**
    (March 4, 1893–March 3, 1897)
25. **William McKinley**
    (March 4, 1897–
    September 14, 1901)
26. **Theodore Roosevelt**
    (September 14, 1901–
    March 3, 1909)
27. **William Howard Taft**
    (March 4, 1909–March 3, 1913)
28. **Woodrow Wilson**
    (March 4, 1913–March 3, 1921)
29. **Warren G. Harding**
    (March 4, 1921–August 2, 1923)
30. **Calvin Coolidge**
    (August 3, 1923–March 3, 1929)
31. **Herbert Hoover**
    (March 4, 1929–March 3, 1933)
32. **Franklin D. Roosevelt**
    (March 4, 1933–April 12, 1945)

33. **Harry S. Truman**
    (April 12, 1945–
    January 20, 1953)
34. **Dwight D. Eisenhower**
    (January 20, 1953–
    January 20, 1961)
35. **John F. Kennedy**
    (January 20, 1961–
    November 22, 1963)
36. **Lyndon B. Johnson**
    (November 22, 1963–
    January 20, 1969)
37. **Richard M. Nixon**
    (January 20, 1969–
    August 9, 1974)
38. **Gerald R. Ford**
    (August 9, 1974–
    January 20, 1977)
39. **James Earl Carter**
    (January 20, 1977–
    January 20, 1981)
40. **Ronald Reagan**
    (January 20, 1981–
    January 20, 1989)
41. **George H. W. Bush**
    (January 20, 1989–
    January 20, 1993)
42. **William Jefferson Clinton**
    (January 20, 1993–
    January 20, 2001)
43. **George W. Bush**
    (January 20, 2001–)

INDEX

★ ★ ★

ABOUT THE AUTHOR

Andrew Santella writes for magazines and newspapers, including *GQ* and the *New York Times Book Review.* He is the author of a number of books for young readers. He lives outside Chicago, with his wife and son.